Charlie, The Awesome Squirrel

A Bushy, Curious Adventure

A children's book filled with adventure, life lessons & respect for leadership and guidance.

by Jermaine L. Stearns

Copyright© 2023 Jermaine L. Stearns. **All rights reserved.**

Charlie the Awesome Squirrel: A Bushy, Curious Adventure
By Jermaine L. Stearns

Cover Design & Book Layout: DCO Branding Agency
Book Editor: Nicole Jackson, Penning His Grace Proofreading and Editing
Book Illustration: Ayan Mansoori & Inspired by Rebecca James

Once upon a time, on a quiet but slightly busy street, in a beautiful place known as Smart Land lived a family of squirrels known as The Awesomes. They lived tucked away in a drey in a huge walnut tree. There was Daddy Awesome, known as Pop, Mom Awesome, the eldest brother John, the middle brother Kenny, and the baby of them all, Charlie, the **curious** one.

The Awesome Family is a family full of love, happiness, excitement, and laughter. But sometimes that happiness was overshadowed by a little bushy mischief. Well, for the most part, Charlie caused a lot of it, and it fell on the rest of the family, but they were always there to pick up the pieces.

Charlie the squirrel wakes up, to the smell of a home cooked breakfast being stirred. Charlie immediately jumps out of bed and runs into the kitchen to see his mother reading **The *Nut Shell News***.

"Good morning, Charlie," his mother said.

"Good morning, Mom," Charlie replied. "How are we feeling today, Charlie?"

"Oh, we are feeling great mom, just great!" "How sweet, baby," Mom Awesome said.

"Mom, what you cooking?" Charlie asked with excitement.

"Just your favorite, baked acorn and sunflower grits, with a glass of roadside water," Mom Awesome said. Charlie jumped up and shouted, **"Y-I-P-P-I! You're the best, Mom!!!"**

"What is all this noise in my sensitive ears?" said a voice coming from down the hall.

"Good morning, Pop!" Mom Awesome & Charlie yelled with smiles on their faces.

"Yea, yea! Good morning to you too," Pop Awesome mumbled with a sour look on his face.

"Charlie, must you wake me up every morning with that noise? Charlie with a mouth full of baked acorns said, **"Sorry, Pop."**

"It's ok son, just make sure you use all that energy up today outside playing," Pop Awesome mumbled. He was still sour from being awakened out of his sleep.

Charlie left the kitchen after putting his meal plate away and went to wake up everyone else in the house. He was always looking for something to keep him occupied and out of trouble. He told himself, "I'll stay inside and play with my siblings." But things did not always go Charlie's way.

"Kenny!" Charlie shouted, while walking down to Kenny's room. **"Kenny!"** Charlie shouted even louder, but there was still no response. Charlie walked into his brother's room and saw a bushy tail staring him in the face.

"No wonder you can't hear me, your tail is listening for you and your head is under the pillow," Charlie said laughingly.

"Kenny, Kenny, Kenny," Charlie is chanting while jumping on his brother's bed.

Without warning, Kenny jumped up and yelled, **"GO AWAY CHARLIE AND LEAVE ME ALONE!"**

"My, aren't we a little nutty this morning! I'm telling mom you yelled at me," Charlie said.

"I don't care, tell mom and I'll tell her you flushed her diamond pecan bracelet down the toilet," Kenny said.

"It was an accident, Kenny, and you know that," Charlie said, tears almost streaming down his furry cheeks. "I was putting my puzzle together in the bathroom as a surprise for Pop when I saw something shiny and couldn't help myself. I went to reach for it, it slipped out of my hand and fell in the toilet. As I was getting down from the counter, my tail hit the toilet bowl switch thingy and down it went. I tried to stop it, but it was too late!"

Kenny replied, "Too bad. If you don't leave me alone, I am going to tell her."

"Fine!" Charlie said. "I will go play with John, since you don't want to play with me."

"John is not there Charlie. He spent the night at the Johnson's house," said Kenny.

"Well since I'm all alone, I will just go outside." Charlie stomped out the door and prepared to go outside.

"Charlie, where do you think you're going mister?" Mom Awesome asked.

"No one wants to play with me, so I thought I'd just go outside and play," Charlie explained.

"Charlie, please listen to me!" Mom exclaimed. "Outdoor is a beautiful place filled with fun and exciting things, but it also can be a dangerous place. You must be careful of the B.T., also known as **BIG THINGS**. They make noise and move on the hot, hard surface. Look out for predators as well. Charlie, please be careful."

"I guess it is time for you to venture outside without your brothers. You are older now, so I have to let you go outside sometimes. You must stay near this tree and never, ever cross the hard surface! "Am I making myself clear?" Mom Awesome stated.

"Yes, ma'am," Charlie responded.

Charlie began to walk towards the upper part of the nest where they entered and exited their home. As he was about to leave, he heard a voice in the distance. **"Be careful Charlie!"** said Pop, who was listening very closely to the conversation that Mom and Charlie had.

"Yes sir, Pop," Charlie said.

"You have until our next-door neighbor, Mr. Reader, pulls in the driveway to be outside. Once you see his car coming, you should make your way back home. Do you understand?" said Pop.

"Yes Sir," yelled Charlie.

It was a bright day, the birds were singing above his head, and Charlie was enjoying the summer breeze that was blowing through his fur. He was excited about being outside all by himself and felt he was on top of the world. Well, from where he was sitting, he was. He was on top of the walnut tree and loved the view.

Charlie sat there wondering if he was going to sit there all day doing nothing or if he would find something or someone to play with. Charlie suddenly heard a strange crunching sound.

"What is that?" Charlie wondered.

Crunch, Crunch, Crunch, the noise sounded again.

"What in the baked acorn is that?" Charlie inquired.

"It's a pecan," the voice said.

"Who is that? Where are you?" Charlie asked.

"It is I, Carter the Great," said the voice.

"Carter the Great? Who is Carter?" said Charlie. He began looking around for this Mr. Great when he suddenly heard a wrestling of the leaves on the walnut tree then out popped a light-brownish squirrel.

"Who are you?" Charlie asked. "It is me, **Carter the Great!**" said Carter.

"Hey, my name is Charlie, Charlie Awesome."

"Nice to meet you. What are you doing up here all by yourself?" said Carter.

"Well, I thought since no one at home wanted to play with me, I would come outside and play by myself. I found myself up here looking at this beautiful view of Smart Land, and those funny, big moving things down there."

"Oh, those are called vehicles," said Carter.

"Vehicles?" asked Charlie. "Yea, those are things that carry people where they need to go," Carter said.

Charlie exclaimed, "Ohhhh, my mother always calls them the B.T.

"B.T.?" Carter asked.

"Yes, Big Things," Charlie said.

"My grandfather, who had a close friendship with a human, said it's called vehicles. The human told him that one day while sitting on the porch," said Carter.

"Wow, your grandfather talked to humans? I thought squirrels were never to have contact with humans?" asked Charlie.

"Yea, that is true, but my grandfather said that all humans are not bad. This human my grandfather talked to was old and lonely. He had no one to talk to, so he talked to my grandfather. Of course, my grandfather didn't talk back, but he just listened," Carter told Charlie.

"Your Grandfather was great!" Charlie said with excitement.

Carter said, "Yea, he was Mr. Wilson the Great! That is our last name you know, **Great!** His father was a great, and his fathers' father was a **Great!** So that makes me **Great** as well," Carter said.

"Just like you, your name is **Awesome**, your dad is **Awesome,** and your dad's dad was **Awesome**, so that makes you **Awesome**. You and I come from a line of **Great** and **Awesome** people," said Carter.

For Carter and me to be around the same age, Carter seemed to be a little wiser than me, but I didn't mind it. I learned a lot from Carter sitting on that branch.

As Carter began to tell Charlie about the pecan, Charlie noticed a Big Thing, pulling up to the neighbor's house. He realized it was time to say goodnight to Carter.

"Carter, I have to go," said Charlie. "Pop said I have to make my way home when Mr. Reader pulls up in his Big Thing, and that is him, Charlie pointed.

"Thank you for talking to me," Charlie told Carter. "I didn't think I was going to find anyone to play with. Maybe tomorrow you can finish telling me about that pecan," Charlie said.

"Sure bud, you're **Awesome**," said Carter! "And you're a **Great** friend," said Charlie.

"See you tomorrow, same place and same time," said Carter.

"Yep, I will be right here," said Charlie.

Charlie jumped down the tree as fast as he could. On his way down, he saw something shiny across the way, but he didn't stop. Charlie figured it would be there tomorrow and he would have something to look forward to exploring with Carter.

Charlie made it home and ran in with excitement to tell his whole family about his day outside, with his new friend Carter. He even told them about the pecan that Carter was eating when the room got silent.

"Pecan?" John said as he came in with an almond muffin in his mouth. "Did he say Pecan mom?" John asked.

Charlie had a strange look on his face because everyone was concerned about the pecan. "Mom, Pop, what is going on?" asked Charlie.

Pop began to tell them the entire story behind the pecan.

"Well Charlie, we don't have pecans on this side of Smart Land.

The only way you get a pecan is to go over to the other side across the hard surface to Smart Land East. We never try to cross the hard surface; it is much **too dangerous! Big Things** make it hard for us to cross the road and sometimes our bush friends don't make it back.

As everyone laid down to go to sleep, Charlie couldn't sleep for thinking about pecans. Charlie was a little scared from the story, but him being Charlie, he wanted to know more.

The next morning, Charlie was allowed to return to the same spot where he met Carter. As he ran up the tree, he stopped to look across the way to see if that shiny figure was in the same spot as yesterday. To his surprise it was still there.

When Charlie reached the top of the tree, Carter was waiting for him.

"Awesome Charlie!" Carter said.

"The Great Carter," Charlie replied.

"I didn't think you were going to make it today," Carter said.

"Yea, I didn't think Pop was going to let me out after that story he told us last night, "said Charlie.

"Story?" asked Carter.

Charlie replied, "Yea, I told him about the pecan. He told me the story of how there were no pecans on this side of Smart *Land, and that I am never to go to Smart La/d East because it is **too** dangerous.

"You're right Charlie," Carter said, "but only the **awesome and great** squirrels are able to go across the road."

"Road?" questioned Charlie.

"Yes road," said Carter.

"From what you told me yesterday, Carter, your grandfather was right," said Charlie.

"We should go," said Carter. "It is bigger and even better than this side of Smart Land. You can get a pecan," Carter said.

"I don't know Carter," Charlie said sadly. "I shouldn't go. My dad said not to."

"Come on Charlie, this will be the biggest adventure and you would really like it," said Carter. **"The taste of that pecan would be bushy cool."**

"Ok, but just as long as we are back before Mr. Reader comes home," Charlie said.

"Deal!!" Carter said with excitement.

As they ventured down and came to the base of the walnut tree about **2 feet away**, Charlie realized that he was close to the hard surface. Charlie became frightened and his tale began to shake. As Charlie and Carter got even closer to the hard surface, they approached with Caution.

"Ok! **Look both ways**," Carter said.

As they both looked to the left and to the right, they did not see anything, especially the vehicles. So, with all their might, they ran as fast as they could to cross the road, **running 8 to 10 miles per hour**. As their tiny little feet reached the green grass, Charlie gave a big sigh of relief and laid on the ground to get a quick rest.

"We made it!" said Carter. **"You sure can run, Charlie!"**

"I had no choice. I want to live to see my second birthday," said Charlie.

They both laughed. While laughing, they found themselves in the middle of a beautiful yard. **Roses, tulips, lilies, dandy lions, fountains, and smooth pathways** were all shaded by the tallest tree they had ever seen --a pecan tree. As they stared at the tree, they noticed a little house on the right side of it with a sign that said, **Jefferson**.

As Carter and Charlie approached the tree, they heard a loud sound coming from the house. It was coming right for them like lightning.

"RUN!" yelled Carter. "What is it?" Said Charlie.

"Run!" Carter yelled, again.

Charlie and Carter took off. As they ran off and looked back, they saw a creature two times their size running full speed ahead after them. It was a dog, a Yorkie named **Jefferson**. He lived there and loved to chase squirrels or anything smaller than him.

Charlie and Carter ran until they realized that Jefferson had stopped chasing them. He couldn't go any further because something was stopping him. Charlie and Carter stopped and stared.

"Boy, that was close," Charlie said.

"Yea, you're right, that was **too close**," said Carter.

"How are we going to get up that tree?" Charlie asked.

"Let's go up the side of the house, jump on a branch, get a pecan, and go back home, "said Carter.

"I like that idea," Charlie said happily.

Charlie and Carter went around the house on the back side, far away from Jefferson. They climbed a ladder that was leaning against the house, jumped on the roof, then onto the pecan tree and up they went. Pecans were **everywhere. Big** ones and **small** ones.

"This must be pecan heaven," Charlie said. "Yea," Carter replied.

"Ok Carter let's get one and get out of here," Charlie said. "Ok, Charlie," Carter replied.

So, they both got **one** pecan each and headed back the same way they *8came to get to the tree. They skedaddled across the rooftop of the house and to the ladder they went, but when they got there the ladder was gone.

"Oh NO!" Cried Charlie. **"It was just here,"** cried Carter.

"What are we going to do now? The only way to get down is to go down the tree and you know who is at the bottom, just waiting on us. **His nose can smell us all the way up here!** "I don't want to die, cried Charlie.

"Ok Charlie, I have a plan," Carter said.

They ran back across the house and onto the pecan tree. Carter's plan was to use himself as a **decoy** for Charlie to get down the tree. So that when Charlie got down, he could easily get away from Jefferson. Carter ran down the tree first and to his surprise, Jefferson was **asleep**. Carter motioned for Charlie to come down and as Charlie was almost to the bottom, Jefferson woke up!

"Run Carter!" Yelled Charlie. "Why?" He asked.

As Carter looked back, Jefferson was after him! Carter took off and when he looked back Jefferson opened his mouth and before he could close it, something yanked him back. **Carter was safe.**

"Yes, yes," jumped Carter. But where was Charlie?

Charlie had jumped onto Jefferson's house and ran down the driveway to the beginning of the hard surface, just in time for the afternoon traffic. Charlie was **frightened** and trying to get back to the other side of Smart Land, but vehicles were everywhere. They were moving fast.

"Charlie don't...," yelled Carter.

But it was too late; Charlie had stepped out in the middle of noon day traffic. As Carter ran to the edge of the road, he did not see Charlie.

"**Oh NO!**" Cried Carter, "what have I done?"

And just when he thought all hope was lost, he saw Charlie doing a **stop, jerk, run, stop, jerk, run** movement in the middle of the road. Charlie was crossing the road! He had one last **stop, jerk, run** and made it back to the other side of Smart Land.

Carter jumped up and down with excitement! But now it was his turn! Carter was not excited about what he had to face. Suddenly a flash of sparkle caught his eye. On the edge of the road near a drain, was a **sparkly pecan bracelet.** As Carter put the bracelet on his arm and looked across the road, he saw what looked like another drain. He jumped down into the hole. As he traveled through, he noticed light coming from the other end, it was the exit to a drain.

When Carter came out of the drain, he immediately called for Charlie.

"Charlie are you ok?" he asked.

"Yeah, I thought I was going to be squirrel stew!" Charlie exclaimed.

"I'm happy that you made it, but please don't ever do that again," Carter said.

"I'm happy too, Carter," said Charlie.

"Hey, look what I found on the other side!" Carter said.

"Wow, that's my mom's pecan bracelet," screamed Charlie.

"It is?" asked Carter.

Charlie began to explain the story of how he lost it two days ago.

"I'm happy you found it," said Charlie. **"You're Great!"**

"You're welcome, and **you're Awesome**," Carter said.

As they went back up the walnut tree, Charlie and Carter talked about their day and how Carter should have listened to Charlie and how Charlie should have listened to his parents. By the time they got to Charlie's house, Mr. Reader pulled into the driveway.

"See you tomorrow, same place and same time?" asked Carter.

"Yep, I will be right there, I think," said Charlie.

Charlie entered the nest and gave his mom her bracelet. He then told them about his adventure. Not knowing what was going to happen, he **apologized** for not listening to what his mom and dad told him about not going over to Smart Land East.

Charlie was given a hug from his dad and a kiss from his mom. They were **happy** just to have him home **safe and sound**.

As Charlie laid down to go to bed for the day, he had a lot of thinking to do about his actions, and all the chores he had to do for the next week, for not listening to his parents. As his dad did the final check before going to bed, he looked in on Charlie.

"Good night, Charlie," Pop said. "Night Pop," said Charlie.

"Remember you are **Awesome!**" said Pop. "Thanks Pop," Charlie said smilingly.

Charlie turned over and drifted off to sleep with a peaceful mind, knowing that he was **awesome**, he has an **Awesome** Family, and he has an **Awesome, Great** Friend.

About the Author

Jermaine L. Stearns (Pastor J,) is a native of Columbia, South Carolina, who currently resides in North Carolina. He holds a Bachelor of Ministry from Andersonville Theological Seminary and serves as the Pastor of Victorious Hope. He is an entrepreneur by way of photography, founder of the JL3 Brand, has served as a mentor for students in Cumberland County Schools, at Fayetteville State University and to local Ministers and Elders in the community. He is most passionate about being a loving husband and a dedicated father.

www.ingramcontent.com/pod-product-compliance
Lightning Source LLC
Chambersburg PA
CBHW050849010526
44107CB00018BA/1225